God's Way of Reading the Bible Through

JESSIE JEAN WEST

authorHOUSE®

AuthorHouse™
1663 Liberty Drive
Bloomington, IN 47403
www.authorhouse.com
Phone: 833-262-8899

Published by AuthorHouse 03/30/2022

ISBN: 978-1-6655-5427-5 (sc)
ISBN: 978-1-6655-5426-8 (e)

Library of Congress Control Number: 2022904564S

Print information available on the last page.

Scripture quotations marked KJV are from the Holy Bible, King James Version (Authorized Version). First published in 1611. Quoted from the KJV Classic Reference Bible, Copyright © 1983 by The Zondervan Corporation.

This book is printed on acid-free paper.

CONTENTS

DEDICATION

To my FATHER GOD, my big brother JESUS CHRIST, my comforter, The HOLY SPIRIT, and my teacher the HOLY GHOST. To my husband, Otis West of thirty two years. To my first born child/and son Adrian, my second born child/and son Derrick, my third born child/ and daughter LaTesha, and my fourth born child/and daughter, Tumeka. Also to my three step children: Betty Ann, Otis Jr., and Douglas. To my twenty-five and plus grandchildren and to my five great grandchildren. To my parents, Elizabeth (L.E.), and Eugene. To my sister, Marsarine, my two brothers: Albert and Robert Charles. To my six step sisters: Carolyn, Mildred; Pamela, Dorothy, Cynthia and Barbara. To all the people in the world. In John 3:16: For God so love the world, that HE gave HIS only begotten SON, that whosoever believeth in HIM should not perish, but have everlasting life. I am saying now, for Jessie so love the people in the world that she is giving and sharing to all, this excellent way of reading the Anointed Word of God. This eighth way was given to me, from GOD, through JESUS by the way of the HOLY SPIRIT. I, like my FATHER, wants everyone to be saved, to come into the knowledge of the truth and none to the lost. So I am writing this GOD Inspired Anointed book to all people, where pen meets paper and I love you all.

ACKNOWLEDGEMENTS

I wish to thank GOD for HIS grace and mercy while writing this book. I know now, without any doubt that GOD's grace is sufficient and HIS mercy endureth forever. I also thank GOD for keeping me, for HE said in HIS WORD: he that hath knowledge spareth his words: and a man of understanding is of an excellent spirit. In other words, a person who knows how to keep his or her cool and to chill. GOD's holy laughter played an important role in my life too. I laughed at all that my FATHER GOD laughs at. This is a great way to rejoice over and over again. Laugh!!!!! A special thanks to my daughter and son for their labors in love. (Tumeka and Adrian). Tumeka for her skills with the computer. Her gift with the illustrations and some art. Adrian for his abilities in some illustrations and his gift in art. I thank also my friend of twenty six years, Luona, for opening her doors so that I could come and take a break and be a blessing.

FOREWORD

I am very well pleased to introduce to all people this new book on how to read the Word of God through. By reading the Bible this way will be easy and also rewarding to all everywhere. The WORD OF GOD will help all of us to grow, to mature and become serious and dedicated students of GOD's WORD. As a Bible Reader, we all will gain so much wisdom, knowledge, instructions and understanding of what GOD is saying to all of us. GOD anointed WORD will reach us all at wherever we are, where we live and also whatever we are doing. The WORD of GOD gives us all insights, information, illuminations and illustrations of our present, past and future lives. As Bible readers we will increase: in faith, in love, in peace, in joy, in anointing, in authority, in might, in power and in manifestation of the glory of GOD, JESUS and the HOLY SPIRIT. In our daily walking with our fingers by turning the pages of the Bible and reading the Old and New Testaments. So then we can run to and fro until all can hear and have heard The Word of God.

PREFACE

In this book, you all will find out one of GOD's purpose in my life. This is to get everyone to become acquainted with GOD, so we all can get too know and meet GOD face to face by reading HIS Word daily. The anointed Word of God will become alive and leap off of the pages into our spirits so that we all can experience so many encounters with GOD through HIS Word. For such a time as this is in the USA, while we are in war, different diseases are being reported on the news. There is terrorism and fear in the land, businesses closing down and going bankrupt, people losing their jobs and homes also. Economy is getting bad for some people. We need the Word of GOD and the HOLY SPIRIT in our lives in order to stay alive, to be in health, to prosper even as our souls prosper. We need God in our lives to make it and to survive. We also need GOD's bread everyday to eat. Give us this day our daily bread. To GOD BE THE GLORY!!!

INTRODUCTION

GOD's Divine Instructions given to me to share and to communicate with all people while I was reading the Bible through for the eighth time. Pen met paper on June 11, 1994 at 12:57 a.m., Saturday morning, to write the sixty six books of the Anointed Word of God down the way God gave them to me to give to all people. Following GOD's divine directions I was told to begin reading the books of the Bible with the smallest number of chapter(s) to the largest number of chapters. Here is GOD's divine order to read the Anointed Word of God through. First I started reading the first five books with one chapter, next the one book with two chapters and then the seven books with three chapters. After that I read all the other books in GOD's Word and I followed the divine pattern GOD gave me. In chapter one I will list all sixty six books in the way that GOD shared with me. So take heed to what you see, hear, taste, touch and say about GOD's Word. Take heed means to listen closely, to pay attention, to hear attentively and to hearken (to hear and obey).

GOD'S WAY OF READING THE BIBLE THROUGH CHAPTER 1

ONE OF GOD'S WAYS
OF READING THE
BIBLE THROUGH

Now this is the way GOD showed me to read the Bible
through for the eighth time. HE said to start reading
the books of the Bible with the least number of chapters
to the books of the Bible with the greatest numbers of
chapters. Here is GOD Special Design Pattern Order for
me to share with all of you:

Jude	I Thessalonians	Revelation
II John	Lamentations	I Kings
III John	I Timothy	Luke
Philemon	Ephesians	Joshua
Obadiah	Galatians	II Samuel
Haggai	Micah	II Kings
II Peter	Song of Solomon	Leviticus
II Thessalonians	Amos	Acts
Zephaniah	Esther	Matthew
Habakkuk	Ezra	I Chronicles
Nahum	Daniel	I Samuel

Joel	Ecclesiastes	Proverbs
Titus	II Corinthians	Deuteronomy
Ruth	Nehemiah	Numbers
Jonah	Hebrews	II Chronicles
Malachi	Zechariah	Exodus
Philippians	Hosea	Job
Colossians	I Corinthians	Ezekiel
II Timothy	Mark	Genesis
I John	Romans	Jeremiah
I Peter	Judges	Isaiah
James	John	Psalms

In this order the first five books only have one chapter. The next book has two chapters. There are seven books with three chapters, six books with four chapters, five books with five chapters, three books with six chapters, one with seven chapters, one with eight chapters, one with nine chapters and two books with ten chapters. Then there are two books with twelve chapters, three with thirteen chapters, two with fourteen chapters, three with sixteen chapters, two with twenty one chapters, two with twenty two chapters, two with twenty four chapters, one with twenty five chapters, one with twenty seven chapters, two with twenty eight chapters and one with twenty nine chapters. These are the one that are left: two with thirty one chapters, one with thirty four chapters, two with thirty six chapters, one with forty chapters, one with forty two chapters, one with forty eight chapters, one with fifty chapters, one with fifty two chapters, one with sixty six chapters and the book of Psalm has one hundred and fifty numbers of Psalms.

Now also let me tell you what the number eight means to me: GOD'S NEW FRESH ANOINTING, GOD'S NEW FRESH FIRE, GOD'S NEW WINE, GOD'S NEW SONG, GOD'S NEW NAME, GOD'S NEW SEASON, GOD'S NEW SPIRIT, GOD'S NEW START, GOD'S NEW THING, GOD'S NEW LIFE, GOD'S DAYS OF HEAVEN ON EARTH, GOD IS WORKING ALL THINGS TOGETHER FOR THE GOOD, THE EIGHT PERSON NOAH, A PREACHER OF RIGHTEOUSNESS, FEW, ALL, NOW and GOD'S NEW BEGINNING for my life.

In II Corinthians 5:17 verse – Therefore if any man be in CHRIST, he is a new creature: Old things are passed away; behold, all things are become new. Behold, I will do a new thing; now it shall spring forth; shall ye not know it? I will even make a way in the wilderness, and rivers in the desert. And we know that all things work together for good to them that love GOD, to them who are the called according to HIS purpose. Romans 8:28 verse. Which sometimes were disobedient when once the long suffering of GOD waited in the days of Noah, while the ark was a preparing, wherein few, that is, eight souls were saved by water. I Peter 3:20 verse. And spared not the old world, but saved Noah the eight person, a preacher of righteousness, bringing in the flood upon the world of the ungodly. Noah means rest. Rest is one of the things GOD is teaching me and wanting me to do now. For me to rest in GOD so I can find the rest of GOD. Do you feel me?

The eighth time reading the WORD OF GOD was quick, short, fast and easy for me as far as time wise is concern. Out of all of the ways GOD has communicated with me to read HIS WORD, this way is very, very special to me because by obeying the voice of GOD, now I am writing this eighth way as my first book. Writing is a gift from GOD to me. Writing is one of GOD's high calling and also one of HIS purpose for my life. This is the first of many books that GOD has put in my heart for me to share with all of you. We are a chosen generation, royal priesthood and a peculiar people of GOD.

Now, I am on my twenty fifth time reading the Anointed WORD of GOD. This twentieth fifth time I call this GOD given way GOD's Supernatural, Extraordinary, Peculiar, Special, Chosen and Favour Way with Great Expectations and Glory Manifested from my FATHER GOD. This way has taken the longest length of time than any of the other twenty four times that I read the WORD of GOD.

I am occupying until GOD sends my big brother JESUS back for us. So this is my occupation now, to be about my FATHER's business. GOD takes care of my business and in return I take care of HIS business. We are partners. We have an awesome partnership together as one.

My request and petition is when you read this part of the book, say these books of the Bible, all sixty six books with the amount of chapters in each one of them like a rap song and with any beat you can make. Remember we have the music on the inside of us. Holler, Holler, back if you can. The rap goes like this. March in place and move your body to the beat. Blow your trumpets (your voices) and sound the alarm (your hands, feet, eyes, heart: your body, soul and spirit, the whole man. Holler! Here we go. You can rap, conversate, reason and chill with GOD by saying these words. You make up your moves, sounds, beats, languages and rhythms unto GOD. Make a joyful noise unto the LORD all ye lands. Holler, holler, back if you can. There are five books with one chapter and they are Jude, II John, III John, Philemon and Obadiah. One with two chapters which is Haggai. Seven books with three chapters – Joel, Titus, Nahum, Zephaniah, Habakkuk, II Peter and II Thessalonians. Ruth, Jonah, Malachi, Philippians, Colossians and II Timothy are the six books with four chapters. In I John, I Peter, Lamentations, James and I Thessalonians there are five chapters in these five books. Six chapters are in these three books; Galatians, Ephesians and I Timothy. Micah with seven chapters, Song of Solomon with eight chapters and Amos with nine chapters. In Esther and Ezra there are ten chapters. Daniel and Ecclesiastes have twelve chapters. In these three books, Nehemiah, II Corinthians and Hebrews there are thirteen chapters. Zechariah and Hosea has fourteen chapters. The three books have sixteen chapters in them, I Corinthians,

Romans, and Mark. Judges and John there are twenty one chapters. Twenty two chapters are in the books of Revelation and I Kings. Luke, Joshua and II Samuel have twenty four chapters. One book with twenty five chapters is II Kings. Leviticus has twenty seven chapters. Acts and Matthew there are twenty eight chapters. Then I Chronicles have twenty nine chapters and the books of Proverbs and I Samuel there are thirty one chapters. The book of Deuteronomy has thirty four chapters. Numbers and II Chronicles there are thirty six chapters. One book with forty chapters is Exodus. One book with forty two chapters is Job. Forty eight chapters in the book of Ezekiel. Genesis has fifty chapters. In the book of Jeremiah there are fifty two chapters. Isaiah has sixty six chapters as unto the Bible with sixty six books. Finally there are one hundred and fifty numbers of Psalms in the book of Psalm. Holler! You all did good. I love you all. GOD is good.

Learn to have fun with the WORD of GOD. Laugh and laugh again. Do you enjoy the holy laughter? Play some games with your husband, wife, children, family friends, co-workers, neighbors and even by yourself if you have too. Go out and purchase some index cards. Buy some white and color ones. Some small and large ones. Write the names of the books of the Bible on one side and number the other side 1-66. Learn to say all the sixty six books of the Bible. To spell all the books of the Bible. To say them from the Old Testament to the New Testament in order and even in alphabetical order. There are thirty nine books in the Old Testament. Twenty Seven books in the New Testament. Make up questions about each book of the Bible that you read. Play the game call baseball. Ask questions and for every correct answer that they give they get to go from one base to another. First base, second base, third base and then home base. Then there is Bible drill.

Each player needs a Bible

One person to be the caller.

The caller names the book of the Bible

The chapters

And the verse.

The first person or persons that find the book, chapters and verse will be the winner.

The caller say attention

Each player stand straight like a soldier:

Draw Sword (Your Bible)

Each player hold his or her Bible in the front of them in one hand

Present Arms

Each player put their other hand on the Bible

Then the caller name the book of the Bible, the Chapters and the verse.

The first person to find what the caller said will be the winner or even winners sometime. An example can be Philippians 4:13 verse–says – I can do all things through CHRIST which strengthen me.

Go to the bank and get a roll of pennies, nickels, dimes, quarters and some dollars if you can. Reward your children with these pennies, nickels, dimes, quarters and even dollars. This money can be put in their piggy banks and even in their bank accounts. Let them earn extra money to buy those expensive tennis shoes, name brand clothes, go to the movies, eat out at their favorite restaurants and for their extra curriculums at school. This can and will be a great tool to teach children and even adults how to be a good steward of GOD's money. We can teach them responsibilities to save, to earn and work for their money. Give them a penny or whatever you choose for every book of the Bible they can name. Also for every book of the Bible they can spell, you choose the amount you want to give them. For your wife husband, family, neighbors, friends and co-workers bake their favorite dessert, cook their favorite meal, buy a gift, send a card or even flowers. These are just some suggestions. You choose, you decide what would be fit, proper and suitable for them from you. We can learn to love GOD's WORD.

We as adults and children can and need to turn off the TVs, radios, CD players, video games, cassette players, DVD and other games and learn to start and continue to spend that good, special precious and quality time with GOD and our family in the WORD OF GOD. THE WORD OF GOD is everlasting. The Anointed WORD of GOD last forever. Do you feel me? Holler back if you can. We can make learning, reading, studying and meditating in and on The WORD of GOD interesting, fun, enjoyable and exciting. GOD is ready and waiting for some of us to come back to HIM and others to come to HIM. One on one. GOD wants all of us to make HIM our first love. We all need to put GOD in first place in our lives.

Here are some scriptures that we can read in the Bible that will show us that the people in the Bible also read the law, GOD's WORD. These verses tell how long they read. Where they read. They also tell us that they meditated, search and study the WORD OF GOD. I believe these scriptures will help and encourage all of us to read, study, meditate and search the WORD of GOD. For all of us to be a student of The Anointed WORD of GOD. We also need a teachable spirit.

Joshua 8:34 verse – And afterward he read all the words of the law, the blessing and cursing, according to all that is written in the book of law.

Deuteronomy 17:19 verse – And it shall be with him, and he shall read therein all the days of his life, that he may learn to fear the LORD, his GOD, to keep all the words of this law and these statutes, to do them:

II Kings 23:2 verse – And the king went up into the house of the LORD, and all the men of Judah and all the inhabitants of Jerusalem with him, and the priests and the prophets and all the people both small and great!

And he read in their ears all the words of the book of the covenant which was found in the house of the LORD.

Nehemiah 8:3 verse – And he read therein before the street that was before the water gate from the morning until midday, before the men and the women, and the ears of all of the people were attentive unto the book of the law.

Nehemiah 8:8 verse – So they read in the book in the law of GOD distinctly, and gave the sense and caused them to understand the reading.

Nehemiah 8:18 verse – Also day by day, from the first day unto the last day, he read in the book of GOD. And they kept the feast seven days; and on the eighth day was a solemn assembly according unto the manner.

Nehemiah 9:3 verse – And they stood up in their place, and read in the book of the law of the LORD their GOD one fourth of the day; and another fourth part they confessed, and worshipped the LORD their GOD.

II Corinthians 3:2 verse – Ye are our epistle written in our hearts, and known and read of all men:

Isaiah 34: 16 verse – Seek ye out of the book of the LORD, and read...

Ephesians 3:4 verse – Whereby, when ye read, ye may understand my knowledge in the mystery of CHRIST.

I Thessalonians 5:27 verse – I charge you by the LORD that this epistle be read unto all the holy brethren.

Revelation 1:3 verse – Blessed is he that readeth, and they that hear the words of this prophecy, and keep those things which are written therein: for the time is at hand.

Jeremiah 36:8 verse – And Baruch the son of Neriah did according to all that Jeremiah the prophet commanded him, reading in the book the words of the LORD in the LORD's house.

Acts 13:15 verse – And after the reading of the law and the prophets the rulers of the synagogue sent unto them, saying, ye men and brethren, if ye have any words of exhortation for the people, say on.

I Timothy 4:13 verse – Till I come, give attendance to reading, to exhortation, to doctrine.

John 5:39 verse – Search the scriptures; for in them ye think ye have eternal life: and they are they which testify of me.

Acts 17:11 verse – These were more noble than those in Thessalonica in that they received the WORD with all readiness of mind, and searched the scriptures daily, whether those things were so.

Psalm 119:148 verse – Mine eyes prevent the night watches, that I might meditate in THY WORD.

Psalm 63:6 verse – When I remember THEE up on my bed, and meditate on THEE in the night watches.

I Timothy 4:15 verse – Meditate upon these things; give thyself wholly to them; that thy profiting may appear to all.

Psalm 143:5 verse – I remember the days of old; I meditate on all THY works; I muse on the work of THY hands.

Joshua 1:8 verse – This book of the law shall not depart out of thy mouth; but thou shalt meditate therein day and night, that thou mayest observe to do according to all that is written therein: for then thou shalt make thy way prosperous, and then thou shalt have good success.

Psalm 1:2 verse – But his delight is in the law of the LORD, and in HIS law doth he meditate day and night.

I Timothy 2:15 verse – Study to show thyself approved unto GOD a workman that needeth not to be ashamed, rightly dividing the WORD of TRUTH.

The number eight also means GOD's Solemn Assembly and GOD's FAVOR.

To GOD be the Glory. Selah. Love!

I Love GOD and all people!

WE CALL THE SHOT! CHAPTER 2

And if it seem evil unto you
to serve the LORD,
choose you this day whom ye will serve;
whether the gods which your
fathers served that were on
the other side of the flood,
are the gods or the Amorites,
in whose land ye dwell:
but as for me and my house,
we will serve the LORD.

Joshua 24:15

WE CALL THE SHOT

The WORD of the LORD said And if it seem evil unto you to serve the LORD, choose you this day whom ye will serve, whether the gods which your fathers served that were on the other side of the flood, or the gods of the Amorites, in whose land ye dwell: but as for me and my house, we will serve the LORD. Joshua 24:15 verse.

This is our choice. Our call and our decision whom this day we will serve. We also can choose, decide and call the shot on how often we will read the WORD of GOD. How much time will we spend reading, studying, meditating and searching the scriptures? Really, getting down to business, will we even take and make the time to spend with GOD in HIS Anointed WORD? We can decide to develop a relationship with GOD. One on one with HIM by talking, reading, praying, sharing and caring just to name a few in such a great and wonderful way. We can have fellowship with GOD everyday of our lives. We can live our lives for GOD everyday and everywhere.

I call heaven and earth to record this day against you that I have set before you life and death, blessing and cursing; therefore choose life, that both thou and thy seed may live; that thou mayest love the LORD thy GOD, and that thou mayest obey HIS voice, and that thou mayest cleave unto HIM: for HE is thy life, and the length of the days: that thou mayest dwell in the land which the LORD swore unto thy fathers, to Abraham, to Isaac, and to Jacob, to give them. Deuteronomy 30:19-20 verses.

In these verses GOD gives us choices and then HE also give us the answer. HE set before us life, death, blessing and cursing and then HE said choose life, that we and our seed may live. What a wonderful and loving GOD we have. Then we need to take responsibility for our actions, choices, calls and decisions.

Here are some ideas, suggestions and places we can read the WORD of GOD: at home, at work (during our break and at lunch time), at a neighbor's house, with friends and family, while waiting for our different doctors appointments, at the beauty and barber shops, while waiting in a long line (such as in a grocery store, department stores, etc), while the children are at practice, at nap time and while we are in the bathroom. These places, suggestions and ideas may or may not work for all of you so then choose others that will work.

Then at the end of the day, we can look back on how, why, where, what, when and with whom we have spent the day. If GOD is left out of that day, this day and any day, then take this word of knowledge and this word of Wisdom from me – We are too, too busy. We have too much on our plates. Our priorities are not in order. Do you feel me? We can start to redeem the time. We can recovery all. And from the days of John the Baptist until now the kingdom of heaven suffereth violence, and the violent take it by force. He that hath ears to hear, let him hear. Matthew 11:12 and 15 verses. Again, we choose, we decide, we call and we all take responsibility for our actions.

If we feed our physical bodies at least three meals a day, then how much more do we need to feed our spirit man the Anointed WORD of GOD. Allow me to give you this idea for a jump start menu for a day or even days. Eat, read and feed on III John for breakfast. Eat, read and feed on III John for lunch. Eat, read and feed on Jude for supper/dinner. Eat, read and feed on Philemon at break time. Eat, read and feed on Obadiah for a bedtime snack. If for one day or night, depending on the time that you sleep or work and you can not get to sleep for whatever reason(s), then eat, read and feed on Haggai. Providing all of this is done in the run of twenty four hours (a day), then you would have read six books and seven chapters in one day. Do you see how easy that can be done? Remember there are 365 days in a year and 366 days in a leap year (that comes every four years).

So please let us designate a set time, a specific time to spend with GOD in HIS WORD. Take a moment, a second, a minute, an hour or even more, but get started this day. The truth of the matter is GOD is worthy of all of our time. (Twenty four/seven) = 24/7, twenty four hours in a day, seven days a week, fifty two weeks in a year, three hundred and sixty five days a year and three hundred sixty six days in a leap year. Do you feel me?

God is waiting. After reading the Bible for a while, we will develop a relationship, friendship and a fellowship with GOD like we never had before with anyone on this earth. We will have a hunger and thirst for GOD that will be filled with unspeakable joy and full of glory that we probably could not even put in words or in any language in the world. So, let us meet GOD face to face on the pages of HIS WORD. Now start loving GOD. GOD is love and love is of GOD. Remember this at all times: GOD loves us as much as HE loves JESUS.

Since we call the shot regarding having GOD in our lives or not, here are some verses in the Bible that GOD has called us and called us to; called us in and called us unto: God of all grace, WHO hath called us unto HIS eternal glory by CHRIST JESUS after that ye have suffered a while, make you perfect, stablish, strengthen, settle you. I Peter 5:10 verse.

According as HIS divine power hath given unto us all things that pertain unto life and godliness, through the knowledge of HIM that hath called us to glory and virtue. II Peter 1:3 verse. You can read II Peter 1:1-12 verses if you like to.

Behold what manner of love the FATHER hath bestowed upon us, that we should be called the Sons of GOD: therefore the world knoweth us not, because it knew HIM not. I John 3:1 verse.

And HE saith unto me, write blessed are they which are called unto the Marriage Supper of the Lamb and HE saith unto me, these are the true saying of GOD. Revelation 19:9 verse.

Who hath saved us, and called us with a holy calling not according to our works, but according to HIS own purpose and grace which was given us in CHRIST JESUS before the world began. II Timothy 1:9 verse

That ye walk worthy of GOD, WHO hath called you unto HIS kingdom and glory.
I Thessalonians 2:12 verse.

And let the peace of GOD rule in your hearts, to which also ye are called in one body; and be ye thankful. Colossians 3:15 verse.

Brethren let every man wherein he is called, therein abide with GOD. I Corinthians 7:24 verse.

GOD is faithful by whom ye were called unto the fellowship of HIS SON JESUS CHRIST our LORD. I Corinthians 1:9 verse.

Unto the church of GOD which is at Corinth, to them that are sanctified in CHRIST JESUS, called to be saints, with all that in every place call upon the name of JESUS CHRIST, our LORD, both theirs and ours. I Corinthians 1:2 verse.

And it shall come to pass that in the place where it was said unto them, Ye are not my people; there shall they be called The Children of the Living GOD. Romans 9:26 verse.

And we know that all things work together for good to them that love GOD to them who are the called according to HIS purpose. Romans 8:28 verse.

For brethren, ye have been called unto liberty; only use not liberty for an occasion to the flesh, but by love serve one another. Galatians 5:13 verse.

There is one body and one Spirit, even as ye are called in one hope of your calling.
Ephesians 4:4 verse.

But when it pleased GOD, WHO separated me from my mother's womb, and called me by HIS grace. Galatians 1:15 verse.

To all that be in Rome, beloved of GOD, called to be saints: Grace to you and peace from GOD our FATHER, and The LORD JESUS CHRIST. Romans 1:7 verse.

Among whom are ye also the called of JESUS CHRIST. Romans 1:6 verse.

May GOD multiply HIS love, peace, grace and mercy to all of us. Selah. Love!!

I Love You God!!

GOD BREATHE
CHAPTER 3

*Then the LORD God formed a man
from the dust of the ground and
breathed into his nostrils the breath of
life, and the man became a living being.*

Genesis 2:7

GOD BREATHE

All scripture is given by inspiration of <u>GOD</u>, and is profitable for doctrine, for reproof, for correction, for instruction in righteousness: That the man of <u>GOD</u> may be perfect, thoroughly furnished unto all good works. <u>II Timothy 3:16-17 verses</u>.

Let me say for example sake, <u>GOD</u> exhale <u>HIS</u> breath on all scriptures in man and now <u>HE</u> is waiting on man to inhale all scriptures in himself and then exhale all scriptures back to <u>GOD</u>. Then would the <u>GOD</u> we say we love, obey, worship and serve be alive? As a parent <u>GOD</u> would love to hear <u>HIS</u> children say to <u>HIM</u> what <u>HE</u> has already said to us. Think about the words that come out of our mouths. Do they line up with the <u>WORD OF GOD</u>? Do they glorify <u>GOD</u>? Do they magnify GOD? Remember we can have what we say. The Bible say that man does not live by bread alone but by every word that proceedeth out of the mouth of <u>GOD</u>. In Proverbs 18:21 verse says Death and life are in the power of the tongue; and they that love it shall eat the fruit thereof. We can speak life to our lives or we can speak death to our lives. What kind of fruit are our tongues speaking? Life or death, which is it? Thou art <u>snared</u> with the words of thy mouth. Snared mean <u>trapped</u> by what you said, <u>ensnared</u> by the words of by our mouth. We are <u>trapped</u> with the words of our mouths. We have been <u>caught</u> with the words we said. <u>Snare – a trapping device</u>. Anything that serves to <u>entangle the unwary</u>. <u>Unwary</u> means – <u>Not alert to danger. Not alert to deception; unguarded.</u> We can have what we say. So let us be mindful and take heed to what we say, what comes out of our mouths. In the book of James says : Out of the same mouth proceedeth blessing and cursing, my brethren these things ought not so to be. You can read the third Chapter of James regarding the tongue, if you like to. For by thy words thou shalt be <u>justified</u>, and by the words thou shalt be <u>condemned</u>. <u>Matthew 12:37 verse</u>.

Remember this, we are to observe, to meditate, to do and let what is written in The <u>Anointed WORD OF GOD</u> come out of our mouths both day and night so is what The <u>LORD</u> said to <u>Joshua</u> and the same words can and do apply to us today. The <u>LORD</u> said to <u>Joshua</u> <u>be strong and of a good courage</u>, only be thou strong and very courageous, that thou mayest observe to do according to all the law. Again, The <u>LORD</u> said to Joshua, be strong and of a good courage; be not afraid, neither be thou dismayed; for The <u>LORD</u> thy <u>GOD</u> is with thee whithersoever thou goest. We see in these verses that The <u>LORD GOD</u> loves us so very much that

HE tells us and reminds us over and over of the same things. GOD knows us very well. GOD knows that we may or may not forget sometimes. The LORD GOD put emphasis on what HE want us to be and to do. GOD adds these adjectives and adverbs to these verbs and nouns. GOD will not tell us to be or to do something that we could not be or could not do. Be strong, Be of a good courage, Be very courageous, only be strong, only be very courageous, be holy, be perfect are some of the things that GOD tells us to be in The WORD OF GOD and the choice will be ours to decide to be obedient to GOD. Remember, in Chapter two, I said We call the shot. We choose, we decide, we call the shot and we take responsibility for our actions.

For The LORD thy GOD is with thee whithersoever thou goest. GOD is omnipresence/omnipresent. GOD is present everywhere at the same time. So do we see why it is so vital important that we all say what GOD say, what GOD said and what GOD is saying. We need to spend quality time with GOD. Time that will cost us something, even if we have to give up something. So I say again, we can have what we say. GOD is longing and waiting for all of us to come together and be as one with HIM.

By getting in GOD's Anointing WORD we can apply all what we learn day by day, week by week, month by month and year by year in our daily walk with GOD. Then when troubles, problems and whatever comes our way, we will know what to do and how to handle them. We also will know how to deal with them. We can let The <u>WORD OF GOD</u> work for us. Let your speech be always with grace, seasoned with salt, that ye may know how ye (You and I) ought to answer every man. <u>JESUS</u> said Be of Good Cheer because <u>HE</u> has overcome the world. The Bible is real and is <u>TRUTH</u>. We can be a witness and a living testimony for <u>GOD</u>. Say ALL is well. Say all things work together for the good of them that love <u>GOD</u> and to them that are the called according to HIS purpose.

Say, I can do all things through <u>CHRIST</u> which strengthens me and all of my needs are met according to <u>HIS</u> riches in glory through <u>CHRIST JESUS</u>. If you want all of your prayers and answers from <u>GOD</u> to be <u>Yes</u> and <u>Amen</u>, then find the promise in <u>GOD's</u> Word and pray those exact words back to GOD and thank GOD in that same prayer. This is <u>TRUTH</u>, according to II Corinthians 1:20 verse - For all the promises of <u>GOD</u> in <u>HIM</u> are Yea, and in <u>Him</u> Amen, unto the glory of GOD by us. <u>Yea</u> - means yes, indeed, truly, agreement, consent, affirmation, not only that, but also, moreover, and in addition to that. <u>GOD</u> is <u>El Shaddai</u>. The <u>GOD</u> that is more than enough. <u>Amen</u> means – so be it, be it so, may it become true, and expression of assent, and expression of approval, and in other word this or that is a <u>Done Deal</u>. Now the prayers must be the promises of <u>GOD</u> in <u>HIM</u>.

These are some of my favorite scriptures: In II Corinthians 1:3 and 4 verses says – Blessed be <u>GOD</u>, even the <u>FATHER</u> of our <u>LORD JESUS CHRIST</u>, the <u>FATHER</u> of mercies and the <u>GOD</u> of all comfort: Who comforteth us in all our tribulation, that we may be able to comfort them which are in any troubles, by the comfort wherewith we ourselves are comforted of <u>GOD</u>. Also in the first Chapter of Ephesians and the third verse says blessed be the <u>GOD</u> and <u>FATHER</u> of our <u>LORD JESUS CHRIST</u>, who hath blessed us with all spiritual blessings in heavenly places in <u>CHRIST</u>.

And let the peace of GOD rule in your hearts, to the which also ye are called in one body; and be ye thankful. Let the <u>WORD</u> of <u>CHRIST</u> dwell in you richly in all wisdom; teaching and admonishing one another in psalms and hymns and spiritual songs, singing with grace in your hearts to The <u>LORD</u>, these verses are found in Colossians 3:15-16.

In Philippians Chapter 4: verses 4-9 are these words: Rejoice in the <u>LORD</u> always: and again I say rejoice. Let your moderation be known unto all men. The <u>LORD</u> is at hand. Be careful for nothing: but in every thing by prayer and supplication with thanksgiving let your requests be made known unto <u>GOD</u>. And the peace of <u>GOD</u>, which passeth all understanding shall keep your hearts and minds through <u>CHRIST</u> <u>JESUS</u>. Finally, brethren, whatsoever things are <u>true</u>, whatsoever things are <u>honest</u>, whatsoever things are just, whatsoever things are pure, whatsoever things are lovely, whatsoever things are of good report; if there be any virtue, and if there be any praise think on these things. Those things, which ye have both learned, and received, and heard, and seen in me, do and the GOD of peace shall be with you. ......but THOU broughtest us out into a wealthy place. Blessed be the LORD, WHO daily loadeth us with benefits.....WHO healeth all thy diseases;..... HE sent HIS WORD and healed them..... Wealth and riches shall be in his house: THOU art my position, O LORD: ..... These also are part of verses in the Bible found in Psalm 66:12 verse, Psalm 68:19 verse, Psalm 103:3 verse, Psalm 112:3 verse, Psalm 119:57 verse are also some of my favorite verses too. My favorite Psalm our of all the one hundred and fifty number of Psalms in The WORD of GOD is Psalm 119:1-176 verses.

This is my favorite verse in The Anointed WORD of **GOD** is Ephesians 3:20 verse - Now unto HIM that is able to do exceeding abundantly above all that we ask so think, according to the power that worketh in us.

All scripture are GOD breathed and they are all inspired by GOD. I want to share this testimony with all of you before I finish Chapter three. The testimony goes like this. We were living in Bossier City, Louisiana and one night I way lying on the floor to spend some quality time with GOD in prayer. So later that particular night I begin praying and after I finished praying I waited to hear from <u>GOD</u>, regarding what I had prayed about. While waiting on <u>GOD</u> I went to sleep and when I woke up, the time on the clock was 4:44 a.m. Then I said to <u>GOD</u>, that <u>HE</u> talked so much that <u>HE</u> put me to sleep. In other words, I was telling <u>GOD</u> that <u>HE</u> talked too much. All of a sudden as soon as those words came out of my mouth, there was an awesome silence, one like I had never witness before in my life even in my spirit. So I layed there so very still on the floor for a while. I believe it was a long while and then I asked <u>GOD</u>, What, what, did I say some thing wrong? What, what, what is it <u>GOD</u>? Then <u>GOD</u> shared with me some awesome words that are sealed in my heart and I will share with you all of some of what <u>GOD</u> told me in he way of two examples. Example #1 – <u>GOD</u> said to me, if <u>I</u> had <u>one hundred children</u> and <u>I (GOD)</u> only hear from <u>seventy</u> of them, only when they are in trouble, when they are sick, when they need money or whatever else they need done in their lives at that given time. Next, are the <u>twenty</u> of <u>HIS</u> children, these <u>GOD</u> only hear from them when they go to church as a part of a religious duty or ritual and when thy come back home, they do whatever and with whomever that pleases them. Then there are the <u>ten</u> children that are left. Those are the ones that truly love <u>HIM</u>. They worship <u>GOD</u> in Spirit and <u>TRUTH</u>. These <u>ten</u> obey and trust <u>HIM</u>. No matter what. According to Nahum 1:7 verse – says-The <u>LORD</u> is good, a strong hold in the day of trouble; and <u>HE</u> knoweth them that trust in <u>HIM</u>. <u>Example #2 –</u> <u>GOD</u> broke this example down even smaller in numbers to make <u>HIS</u> words clear to me. <u>God</u> said if <u>HE</u> had only <u>ten children</u> and <u>GOD</u> only hear from <u>seven</u> of them when they needed something from <u>HIM</u>. These <u>seven</u> were too busy doing their own thing. Next the <u>two children</u> that had the form of godliness and denying the power of <u>GOD</u>. Then there is the <u>one</u> child, <u>GOD</u> said that love, obey, worship and honor <u>HIM</u> always. Ask ourselves this question, what <u>child</u> am I? I cried and wept so much after all what <u>GOD</u> told me that night. I know from being a parent of four children this is an awesome responsibility. <u>GOD</u> is a better parent than all of us put together. Just to think that <u>HE</u> has to put up with all of us. And some of us have the nerve to talk about the children of Israel.

If we are not where we need and want to be with <u>GOD</u>, then repent. Ask <u>GOD</u> for forgiveness and amend our ways. Get our lives right with <u>GOD</u>. Start a new life with <u>GOD</u> being in control, in charge, and in first place. Began again!!! Be all what <u>GOD</u> want us to be. Fulfill <u>God's</u> purpose in our lives. Reach our destiny and understand our potential. I also told <u>GOD</u> to take a rest, a long rest after dealing with all of us that are <u>HIS</u> children now and the ones that will become <u>HIS</u> later on and if there are those who choose not to be <u>HIS</u> children a rest from them also. I also told <u>GOD</u> that I did not know whether is was scriptual for a child to tell her <u>FATHER</u> what to do and even if the parent would obey. I reminded HIM that HE rested on the seventh day after the creation and now again HE needed to rest from all of us.

After all of that, I told HIM, that I would never tell HIM that HE talks too much. Since that day, I have never let those words come out of my mouth again. I thank GOD after that encounter with HIM for giving me opportunities to hear HIS WORDS at anytime, any place, anywhere and with any body, especially with HIM, one on one. Just HIM and I. As a result from that experience, I continue to thank HIM for choosing to speak to me. I shared with GOD that whenever HE need, want, desire, delight and have pleasure to speak HIS WORD that I am available and a yielded daughter to listen, to hear and hearken (hear and obey) HIS voice. I say speak on and say on DADDY.

For all of GOD's children that are: too busy, rebellious, in sin, hardheaded, stiffnecked, disobedient, selfish, in witchcraft, all of them that GOD only hear from when they are in trouble, in debt, sick, need money, ill, all of them that goes to church as a ritual, as a religious duty; or what have you, those who go back home and do whatever pleases themselves. Lip servicers and not from the hearts. Those who comes to GOD only when they need something, those who has the form of godliness and denying the power of GOD. To all of the other children of GOD that are not doing what HE said, is saying and will say to do. Those who do not line their lives up with HIS WORD and if I left out any – YOU TOO!!! GOD KNOWS. I said like Isaiah said, Here am I. I delight myself in GOD, in HIS WORD, in HIS HOLY SPIRIT and in HIS HOLY GHOST.

In the year 2000, GOD said to me: Be Quiet, Be Silent, Be Still and know that I am GOD. When I pray now in the Spirit, in my heavenly language, in tongues, I told GOD that I wanted all of those prayers and groanings to say, when those words leave my lips, tongue, voice, mouth and heart and reaches HIS ears I want the HOLY SPIRIT of GOD to interpret and make intercessions for me of my prayers to say, I Love You, I Love You, over and over again to my FATHER. So from that day forward, when I pray in the Spirit, in tongues, in my heavenly language and in groanings, I say to GOD, I Love You. All of you who know me now and all of you who will get to know me, know now and will know that this is a pleasure for me to pray these kind of prayers. My FATHER is well-pleased with me when I pray these particular prayers. As they enter in HIS ears, HE enjoys hearing me say, I Love You, I Love You, over and over again, instead of hearing me murmuring, grumbling and complaining. Do you feel me? Can you relate to what I am saying, even if you are not a parent? My FATHER delights HIMSELF in hearing those sweet smelling savor wonderful aroma words in HIS ears, mouth and nostrils. All of me bless GOD in whatever I do say, hear, taste, touch and all that

I might even have left out of this sentence. GOD knows, even if all of you do not understand what I am saying and writing with this black pen, with this black ink that is meeting this white paper on this first day of the fifth month in the year two thousand and three at 12:57 p.m., in the afternoon, while I am sitting in the den in my recliner chair and listening to the T.V. at the same time.

I recall these verses in the Bible, in the book of Revelation, these are the words: And the four beasts had each of them six wings about HIM; and they were full of eyes within: and they rest not day and night, saying, Holy, holy, holy, LORD GOD Almighty, which was, and is, and is to come. And when those beasts give glory and honour and thanks to HIM that sat on the throne, who liveth for ever and ever, the four and twenty elders fall down before HIM that sat on the throne, and worship HIM that liveth for ever and ever and cast their crowns before the throne, saying, THOU art worthy, O LORD, to receive glory and honour and power: for THOU has created all things, and for THY pleasure they are and were created and I beheld, and I heard the voice of many angels round about the throne and the beasts and the elders. And the number of them was ten thousands of thousands; Saying with a loud voice, Worthy is the LAMB that was slain to receive power and riches, and wisdom, and strength, and honour, and glory, and blessing. And every creature which is in heaven, and on the earth, and under the earth, and such as are in the sea, and all that are in them, heard I saying, Blessing, and honour, and glory, and power, be unto <u>HIM</u> that sitteth upon the throne, and unto the <u>LAMB</u> for ever and ever. And the four and twenty elders fell down and worshipped <u>HIM</u> that liveth for ever and ever.

As you read, study, search and meditate all the scriptures written in the Bible you can have <u>The Living Bread</u> and <u>The Living Water Banquet Feast</u> like as unto <u>The Buffet Style</u>. At this Feast we can eat and drink all we want too. The Living Water and The Living Bread Banquet Feast will never run out or even get empty. This <u>Feast</u> can and will last forever. You will see yourselves in GOD's Anointed WORD as you spend time with GOD in reading The Bible through. We can use this as <u>The Tool</u> in a great and excellent way to spread The Gospel/The Good News to everyone. We also can be a witness to Jerusalem, Judah, Samaria and to the uttermost part of the earth. (To the people in the whole world). In other words – to our families, neighbors, friends, co-workers, strangers, people we meet from city to city, town to town, rural areas to rural areas, state to state and country to country. Everywhere. Remember we are the <u>salt</u> of the earth and the <u>light</u> of the world.

<u>GOD</u> want all of us to have eternal lives. <u>GOD</u> want us to know also that <u>HE</u> loves us as much as <u>HE</u> loves <u>JESUS</u>. So I encourage, exhort, compel, command, beseech,

plead and beg all of us with the power that is invested in me from my <u>FATHER GOD</u>, for all of us to read, study, meditate and search all scriptures (The Bible) in order for us to survive, to stand and to make it <u>in such a time as this</u>. I say to all without <u>GOD, JESUS CHRIST</u> and The <u>HOLY SPIRIT</u> in us and working through us, we will not last. <u>GOD</u> said "<u>I AM That I AM</u>".

Selah. Love!!!
I Love <u>GOD</u> and all of you!!!

PEN MEETS PAPER
CHAPTER 4

My heart is stirred by a noble theme
as I recite my verses for the king;
my tongue is the pen of a skillful writer.

Psalm 45:1

PEN MEETS PAPER

O taste and see that <u>The LORD</u> is good: blessed is the man that trusteth in <u>HIM</u>.
<u>Psalm 34:8 verse</u>

My heart is inditing a good matter: I speak of the things which I have made touching the King; <u>my tongue</u> is <u>the pen</u> of a <u>ready writer</u>. <u>Psalms 45:1 verse</u>

Pen met paper on June 11, 1994 at 12:57a.m., on a Saturday morning to write one of <u>GOD's</u> Ways in which to read the Bible through. So I wrote <u>The Eighth Way</u> out on two pieces of paper and gave them out to some family members, friends and some church members. Later on I had them typed and pass them out to other people this time. Now, once again <u>pen met paper</u> on March 9, 2003, Sunday night at 7:57 p.m., <u>God</u> gave me this dream, idea and vision to write this Eighth Way of reading <u>HIS WORD</u> in a book to all people.

And The <u>LORD</u> answered me, and said; write the vision, and make it plain upon tables that he may run that readeth it. For the vision is yet for an appointed time, but at the end it shall speak, and not lie: though it tarry, wait for it; because it will surely come. It will not tarry.....but the just shall live by his faith. Habakkuk 2:2-3 and 4b verses.

The favour of The LORD is in and on this book. To everyone that read this love book and love letter to my FATHER will run and encourage all people to read The WORD of GOD. This book and every book that I write, I want everyone to know this: that GOD, JESUS CHRIST, THE HOLY GHOST and the HOLY SPIRIT are my partners. My heart, eyes, ears, tongue, hands, feet, in other words all of me, my complete man (body, soul, and spirit) are continually open to hear the voice of GOD in what to share with all people.

In the book of John, chapter three and verse sixteen say – For God so loved so loved the world, that HE gave HIS only begotten SON, that whosoever believeth in HIM should not perish, but have everlasting life. So I, Jessie Jean, (GOD's baby girl) HIS baby daughter) so loved the world that I give this GOD's vision, dream and idea to all people to read The WORD of GOD daily. I say to all people Time Out NO Excuse. Everyone (all people) need GOD and HIS Anointed WORD in order to live. For in HIM we live, and move, and have our being; as certain also of your own poets have said, for we are also HIS offspring. Acts 17:28 verse.

Now as I look back and reflect on my life, I see why writing is one of my gift and passion. Writing is something I enjoy doing. When I am watching T.V., I find myself getting a pen or pencil taking notes and writing on magazines, newspapers, tablets and loose paper or whatever I can find to write on. While I was in school, I was elected to be the secretary in different curriculums, clubs and after school activities. During my young adult life, I was chosen and elected to be secretary, president, treasurer and even the church clerk in different auxiliaries and departments of the church.

From time to time I read about Ezra, Baruch, Seraiah, Shera, Shebna, Shaphan, Shavsha, and Shimshai, the scribes in the Bible. Also Jonathan, David's uncle, was a counselor, a wise man, and a scribe. Ezra was the priest, the scribe, even a scribe of the words of the commandments of the <u>LORD</u>, and of <u>HIS STATUTES</u> to Israel. These Scribes are a great inspiration to and for me while writing this book and the other books that GOD has birth in my spirit. I am so very thankful and grateful to <u>GOD</u> for putting and placing <u>HIS</u> Anointed dreams, visions, ideas, plans and thoughts on the inside of me to fulfill <u>HIS</u> high calling and purpose in my life by writing this book and other books to come.

While writing this book I am learning to trust and have faith in <u>GOD</u> in a higher dimension and a closer encounter with <u>HIM</u> like I have never experience before in my fifty three years of living. <u>GOD</u> is teaching me how to write in <u>HIS</u> love as <u>HIS</u> presence covers these pages. I appreciate <u>GOD</u> for giving me a teachable spirit.

Now that pen and paper has met it is time that they get married. The <u>LORD</u> my <u>GOD</u> is teaching me to profit and HE is leading me in the way I should go. The <u>LORD</u> my <u>GOD</u> is giving me power to get wealth, that HE is establishing <u>HIS</u> covenant which <u>HE</u> swore unto our fathers, as it is this day. Godliness is profitable unto all things, having promise of the life that now is and of that is to come. This is a faithful saying and worthy of all acceptation. Meditate upon these things; give thyself wholly to them; that thy profiting may appear to all.

This is a faithful saying, and these things I will that thou affirm constantly, that they which have believe in <u>GOD</u> might be careful to maintain good works. These things are good and profitable unto men. <u>GOD</u> blesses me to prosper, to be in health even as my soul prospereth. This gift <u>GOD</u> has given me to write is very precious. Wherever <u>GOD</u> sends this book and other books, they will prosper. This is one of GOD's ways that HE has provided for me to prosper and have good success. I believe in <u>GOD</u>, therefore I am establish (kept safe). I also believe in <u>GOD's</u> prophets so shall I prosper. I am prospering now and I will continue to prosper in The <u>LORD</u> my <u>GOD</u>.

My delight is in <u>The WORD of GOD</u>, in <u>HIS WORD</u> do I meditate day and night and whatsoever I doeth shall prosper. <u>GOD</u> has anointed my hands to write about <u>HIM</u> and <u>HIS LOVE.</u> <u>GOD</u> knows that I love HIM and <u>HIS</u> WORD more than my food that I eat. One of my grand daughter tells me very often, "Maw Maw, you are rich in The <u>LORD</u>. This is a true saying and is the truth. I do not put no limits on my <u>FATHER</u>. In <u>GOD's WORD</u> you will find these words. But as it is written, eye hath not seen, ear hath not heard, neither have entered into the heart of man, for the things which <u>GOD</u> hath prepared for them that love <u>HIM</u>. Again, I say <u>GOD</u> knows that I love <u>HIM</u> so very, very much.

Sometimes I get so caught up in <u>GOD</u>, in <u>HIS WORD</u>, in praying, in studying, in meditating, in reading, in writing and in searching the things of <u>GOD</u> that I have to tell myself, that I have other things to do. I am doing these things and those things that pertain to <u>GOD's</u> business make them so easy for me to do a 24/7, just <u>GOD</u> and Me. One with one and one on one.

Can you imagine how big and thick the Bible would be if all of what JESUS did in those thirty three and a half years on earth were written in The WORD of GOD? Put your imagination to Work. How many of us would it take to lift and even pick up the Bible if this was so? In John 21:25 verse says - And there are also many things which JESUS did, the which, if they should be written every one, I suppose that even the world itself could not contain the books that should be written. Amen. So let all of us lift up JESUS so that GOD will draw all men unto HIMSELF.

This is another person in the Bible named Enoch. Enoch walked with GOD after he begat Methuselah three hundred years and begat sons and daughters. Can you imagine what kind of rap sessions and chilling time Enoch and GOD had together? What about the time Enoch spent with Methuselah and taught him, his other brothers and sisters? Enoch walked with GOD: and he was not; for GOD took him. Methuselah lived nine hundred and sixty nine years. What if all the days of Methuselah life (969 years) was recorded in the Bible on what he learned from his father about what he and GOD talked about. Then how large would the Bible be? From time to time when a year comes and go (365 days), I think about Enoch, that lived three hundred and sixty five years (365 years). You can read the fifth chapter of Genesis, if you'd like to.

One day I wrote down some things that I wanted to do, to study and to learn about in the Bible. I did this in an outline form. This took me having to use six A's and six Z's (AAAAAA to ZZZZZZ). Then I said to myself, there is got to be more alphabets than the twenty six letters that we have now. This would not take me long to write up 150 too 200 pieces of paper to share with you all about GOD, what GOD is doing, have done and what GOD will do and continue to do for me and for all of us because HE love us so very much. I say again, that GOD loves us as much as <u>HE</u> loves <u>JESUS</u>. I believe that it would be safe to say, that we can not plant enough seeds, grow enough trees, make enough paper and make ink to write all about <u>GOD, JESUS CHRIST, HOLY SPIRIT,</u> HOLY GHOST and all the angels <u>GOD</u> has given and assigned to all of us.

I love all of <u>GOD's WORD</u>. All of HIS WORD are my favorite. But if I had to choose out one verse to say that my favorite verse, I believe this would be the one. <u>Now</u> into <u>HIM</u> that is able to do exceeding abundantly above all that we ask or think according to the power that worketh in us. I want to share this revelation <u>GOD</u> told me about the word <u>NOW</u>. <u>GOD</u> said to turn that word <u>now</u> around and the word now spells <u>WON</u>. <u>GOD</u> said you <u>won now</u>. This is a win-win situation in all things <u>HE</u> does in my life. So I take heed when I see the word now in the Bible. <u>Now</u> I say, Jessie won now because <u>GOD</u> is able to do exceeding abundantly above all that Jessie ask or Jessie think according to the power that worketh in Jessie because Jessie has the power of <u>GOD</u> working in her. Make <u>GOD's</u> WORD personal for you too.

Finally before I end this chapter I want to share with all of you <u>some</u> of the <u>assignments</u> that <u>GOD</u> has given me when pen met paper.

1. <u>GOD</u> said at 12:04 a.m., 5/18/96, Saturday morning for me (Jessie Jean West) to write 21 pages of this verse Psalm 115:14 verse.

2. <u>GOD</u> said on 5/6/95, Saturday morning at 1:03 a.m. - to write 7 pages of this verse Psalm 138:8 verse.

3. <u>GOD</u> said to write Joshua 1:5 verse 1,000 times and say the verse also - on 3/30/95 - Thursday night at 7:55 p.m.

4. <u>GOD</u> said to write Deuteronomy 30:19 verse 100 times and to say this verse also. – on 4/13/95 – Thursday night at 11:17p.m. The finish date is 6/4/96 Tuesday night at 9:45p.m.

5. <u>GOD</u> said to write 10 pages of these verses and to say them. Deuteronomy 28:1-14 verses – 4/13/95 Thursday night at 11:11 p.m. and my finish date is 5/8/96 - Wednesday night at 11:11 p.m.

6. <u>GOD</u> said to write 10 pages of these verses and say them, on 4/13/95 at 11:20 p.m. Joshua 1:3,4,6,7,9 and 11 verses.

Examples I wrote these verses:

1. Joshua 1:5 verse - There shalt not any man be able to stand before the (OJADLT) all the days of thy (OJADLT) life: as I was with Moses so I will be with thee (OJADLT). I will not fail thee (OJADLT) nor forsake thee (OJADLT).

2. <u>Psalm 112:3 verse</u> - wealth and riches are in my (OJADLT) house: and HIS righteousness

endureth forever. The initials O.J.A.D.L.T. stands for Otis, Jessie, Adrian, Derrick, La Tesha, and Tumeka.

These are my children favorite verses when they were young.

1. <u>Adrian – Psalm 100:1 verse</u> - Make a joyful noise unto the <u>LORD</u>, all ye lands.
2. <u>Derrick</u> – Philippians 4:13 verse – I can do all things through <u>CHRIST</u> which strengtheneth me.
3. <u>La Tesha - Exodus 20:12 verse</u> - Honour thy father and thy mother: that thy days may be long upon the land which the LORD thy GOD giveth thee.
4. <u>Tumeka - Hebrews 11:1 verse –</u> Now faith is the substance of things hoped for, the evidence of things not seen.

May <u>GOD's</u> grace be with you all. I salute and love all of you. Selah.

I LOVE GOD!!!!

THE WORD
CHAPTER 5

For the word of God is alive and active.
Sharper than any double-edged sword,
it penetrates even to dividing soul and
spirit, joints and marrow; it judges the
thoughts and attitudes of the heart.

Hebrew 4:12

THE WORD

For **The WORD of GOD** is quick, and powerful, and sharper than any two edged sword, piercing even to the dividing asunder of soul and spirit, and of the joints and marrow, and is a discerner of the thoughts and intents of the heart. <u>Hebrews 4:12 verse</u>

We are bless when we seek The LORD with our whole heart and keep <u>HIS</u> testimonies. We must keep <u>GOD's WORD</u> diligently as <u>HE</u> directs our ways. Also we need to take heed to <u>The LORD GOD WORD</u> as <u>HE</u> teaches us so we want sin against <u>HIM</u>. We can meditate, rejoice, have respect and delight ourselves in <u>GOD's Anointed WORD</u>, so we will not forget what <u>HE</u> is Saying to us. WE also can pray to <u>GOD</u> to open our eyes so we can behold <u>HIS</u> handiwork in <u>HIS WORD</u>. <u>The LORD WORD</u> can be our counselors, our teachers to make us understand, to strengthen us, to quicken us so we can declare <u>HIS</u> wondrous works. Then we can choose the way of truth, <u>HIS TRUTH</u> is HIS WORD. Let us observe <u>The Bible (GOD's WORD)</u> With our whole heart so we can learn HIS righteous judgments. <u>GOD's</u> judgments are good. We can be companion with all of them that respect, honor, obey, fear GOD and keep HIS WORD. The earth is full of The LORD's mercy and HE teaches us HIS WORD. Let HIS tender mercies come unto us that we may live. GOD WORD is a lamp into our feet and a light unto our path so let us refrain our feet from every evil way and keep GOD's WORD. Know that HE is our hiding place and our shield and we have hope in The LORD's WORD. So love GOD's WORD.

Ask GOD to deliver us, to uphold us, to have dominion over us and to order our steps in HIS WORD. The LORD WORD is very pure. When we cry unto The LORD with our whole heart, ask GOD to save us and give is understanding so we can live. The righteousness of HIS testimonies is everlasting. We can have great peace because we love GOD's Word and nothing shall offend us. Please let our lips speak praises to GOD as HE teaches us in HIS WORD. In Psalm 19:verse 14 says – Let the words of my mouth and the meditation of my heart be acceptable in THY sight, O LORD, my rock and my Redeemer. Now our meditation of GOD shall be sweet and we will be glad in The LORD. Then we can let our mouths speak of wisdom and the meditation of our heart shall be of understanding.

In Galatians 6:6 verse – say Let him that is taught in The WORD communicate unto him that teacheth in all good things. So let me communicate with all of you to give you all a Sneak Preview of these other ways <u>GOD</u> has birth in my spirit to read <u>HIS WORD</u>.

Pen met paper on January 24, 1999 at 9:30a.m. until.... These Bible Reading Ways was written at church while the Pastor is reviewing the Sunday School Lesson. – Subject - Forgiving Each Other. Matthew 18:21-35 verses is the scripture reading. <u>R.T.B.T.</u> stands for <u>R</u>eading <u>T</u>he <u>B</u>ible <u>T</u>hrough.

1. 22nd time R.T.B.T. = Read in Alphabetical Order.
2. 23rd time R.T.B.T. = Read start with the largest to the smallest
3. 24th time R.T.B.T. = Read the books of the Bible with the letters in my household and my mother, brother, sister and cousin Martha and then the smallest book to the largest. The letters O.J.A.D.L.T.E.A.R.M. stands for <u>O</u>tis, <u>J</u>essie, <u>A</u>drian, <u>D</u>errick, <u>L</u>aTesha, <u>T</u>umeka, <u>E</u>lizabeth, <u>A</u>lbert, <u>R</u>obert, <u>M</u>arsarine and <u>M</u>artha, my cousin.
4. 25th time R.T.B.T. = Read from Malachi to Genesis and from Revelation to Matthew.
5. 26th time R.T.B.T. = Read from <u>Z</u> to <u>A</u> (The book of the Bible that start with the letter <u>Z</u> to the letter <u>A</u>)
6. 27th time R.T.B.T. = Read the smallest book in alphabetically order to the largest one.
7. 28th time R.T.B.T. = Read the largest book in alphabetical order to the smallest one.

8. 29th time R.T.B.T. = Read the Bible as led by the <u>HOLY SPIRIT</u> (as I open the Bible up).

9. 30 time R.T.B.T. = Read the first book of the Bible that is in my spirit or the first one I hear on T.V., on a Christian program, a tape, radio, or through or by conversation - After reading the last book from the 29th time. Whatever or whomever comes first, this will be my choice. HOLY SPIRIT, HOLY GHOST I need your help, to bring this to my remembrance.

10. 31st time R.T.B.T. = Pen met paper again on October 12, 2000, Thursday morning when I looked at the clock it was 10:19 a.m. This is the way I received from <u>GOD</u> on how to read the Bible through for this 31st time. <u>HE</u> said to start with the smallest books of the Bible like on the Eighth time. Or at random or while studying with reading what chapter or last chapter or whatever chapter with the last word and begin reading backward the whole chapter, book and to mark them as I go. Also, I can keep a record or not. GOD will and my assigned angel will keep a record.

By getting to know <u>GOD</u> and <u>HIS WORD</u>, I have learned how to pray. What to pray and who to pray for. How to be a great prayer warrior, a good intercessor and how to speak. How to answer every man by letting my speech be always with grace, and seasoned with salt. I learn to speak to myself in Psalms, hymns, spiritual songs, singing and making melody in my heart to the <u>LORD</u>. To let the <u>WORD</u> of <u>CHRIST</u> dwell in me richly in all wisdom teaching and admonishing one another in psalms and hymns and spiritual songs, singing with grace in my heart to the LORD. How to encourage my own self. To cast all my care upon <u>God</u>, for HE careth for me. To be clothed with humility and having on the whole armor of <u>GOD</u>. Having a honest and good conversation and my works with meekness of wisdom. To receive with meekness the engrafted <u>WORD</u>, which is able to save our souls.

To Discern, to know the truth from a lie, regardless of whose mouth the words come out of. To guard my heart. To be a hearer and a doer of <u>GOD's Anointed Word</u>. To Be quiet, silent, and still and know <u>GOD</u> is <u>GOD</u>. There is so much, much more that will take a life time to tell all of what <u>GOD</u> has revealed to me, HIS baby Daughter.

Finally pen met paper and they got married. Till the next book is written remember this that I Love You All.

P.S. I Love You <u>DADDY</u>. Every book that I write is a Love Letter/Love Book To my <u>FATHER GOD</u> to thank <u>HIM</u> for The LoveLetter/LoveBook – The Bible that HE gave to us all.

Selah. Love!!!!! I LOVE YOU <u>GOD</u>!!!!!

Printed in the United States
by Baker & Taylor Publisher Services